NEVER EN

A Recovery Workbook for Addictions, Obsessive Compulsive Behaviors & Eating Disorders

by Nina Bingham

All Rights Reserved

Published by Irving Street Press

Dedication

To my daughter Moriyah, may you and your generation be free from self-defeating patterns. May you find a way to let your magnificent light so shine that you will never have to walk in the darkness of addiction.

Table of Contents

Preface: What This Workbook Can Do For You

This workbook is recommended for recovery from: Alcohol Abuse or Addiction, Drug Abuse or Addiction, Sex/Porn Addiction, Smoking, Gambling, Eating Disorders, Hoarding, Shoplifting, Obsessive-Compulsive Disorders, PTSD/Trauma, and other addictive and compulsive behaviors.

Health Precautions: If you are experiencing substance addiction, an eating disorder, Obsessive-Compulsive Disorder or behaviors, an impulse-control disorder (hoarding, shoplifting, sex/porn addiction, gambling, etc.), Post-Traumatic Stress Disorder or another mental health problem such as depression or anxiety, be advised that this workbook was created as an adjunct to psychotherapy, and not intended as the sole source of treatment. A mental health professional should be consulted to provide thorough assessment, diagnosis and treatment of mental health concerns. This workbook is a supplementary tool to guide you in your personal quest for mental health, but should not be the primary means of mental healthcare.

This psychotherapeutic workbook is designed to benefit you in the following ways:

(1) Understand the Root Causes of the Addictive or Obsessive Thinking

(2) Acceptance of Death: Peace Instead of Fear

(3) Develop Higher Frustrational Tolerance: Refrain from Catastrophizing

(4) Uncovering Absolute Thinking: Refusing "All or Nothing" Thinking, and Adopting a More Flexible, Alternative-Friendly Existence

(5) Refusing Perfectionism-Recognition of Grandiose Expectations of Self and Others

(6) Disputation of Negative Beliefs-ABCDs of Addictive Thinking to Dispute Negative Beliefs

(7) Identify Emotional Thinking vs. Rational Thinking

(8) The Grief Process: Working through Grief/Losses of the Past

(9) Trauma Recovery: Identifying Resentments and Regrets, and Finding Liberty from Losses

(10) Understand Post-Traumatic Growth

(11) Narrative Therapy: Telling Your Unique Story

(12) Inner-Child Therapy and Re-Parenting-Working with Your Inner Child

(13) Forgive and Remember: Forgiveness of Self and Others

(14) Lapse Prevention: Urge-Surfing Technique

(15) Crisis Kit-Management of Crisis Moments

(16) Body Speak: Exercises that Create More Body Awareness

(17) Environmental Awareness: Mindfulness Training

(18) The A-C-C-E-P-T Method: Re-Designing Your Life

(19) Reflections of My Journey: Reflect on the Growth You've Experienced in Your Journey of Recovery.

Introduction

I cannot stress this sentence enough: When you are in the process of healing, you must give yourself permission to take time out to focus on your recovery. Think of it this way: if a loved-one were in the hospital recovering, but kept getting out of bed to walk on a broken leg, how long do you think it would take for the leg to heal? Likewise, if you're in recovery, you are just like that hospital patient: you would benefit by making healing a priority, and set some time aside to use the self-intervention exercises and coping strategies in this book. If you don't, you will not be caring for yourself, and healing could take a very long time.

We over-drink, over-drug, over-eat, etc. at the expense of doing other more constructive things. It is excess of the behavior, and a lack of control that defines addiction. Like the title of this workbook says, when it comes to our preferred addiction, it's never enough, and the truth is, it never will be. We become dependent on the stimulus for our happiness. Addiction is both a physical problem (addictive cravings and withdrawal symptoms), as well as a psychological dependency. "Alcohol intoxication is also a defense, anesthetizing the individual from the painful aspects of suppressing the true self. Alcohol intoxication can soothe the anxiety related to independent strivings and promote an illusory sense of autonomy and freedom" (Sacks, 2003).

Recovery is realizing our unique potentials apart from the addiction, and claiming that possibility as our own. Recovery is making a choice to expand instead of contract, to reach for and risk for our goals, so we can create a life of freedom: freedom from bondage to obsessive thoughts and compulsive actions. We are ultimately free when we are free not to choose the addiction.

It is my hope you will see the journey of recovery as a possibility for yourself in the beginning, which grows into a probability, and then blossoms into a certainty. If you will put yourself where fate can meet you, smack dab in the company of others who are scaling mountains, I promise you'll find the climb much easier and even encouraging. If you're going to scale the mountain of addictive or obsessive and compulsive behaviors, it's best to not attempt it alone. Climbers "tether up" for a good reason: so when one climber slips and falls, the others can keep them safe.

I wish for you that this "mountain climbing map" will deliver you safely to your recovery goals. Only an "old hand" climber knows all the tricks and nuances of mountain climbing, so believe me when I say, you're with an experienced Sherpa. I've walked up and down my share of medical and psychological mountains, and have risen to the challenge only because I have others to lean on.

We can do this together,

Nina Bingham

Portland, Oregon 2012

PART 1: Mind Awakening

Chapter 1. The Three Fears: The Roots of Addiction, Obsessive-Compulsive Behavior and Eating Disorders

Throughout psychology's history there have been many theories as to why people become addicted. I'm going to present three theories, or explanations, for the problem. I'm not claiming that I prefer one theory over another; in fact, all three explanations seem valid to me. Maybe you'll relate to one more than the others, or maybe none of these theories will resonate with you. But I wanted to give you a little "food for thought" about why addictions are so prevalent and universal in human behavior.

Fear of Death

"There are only two sure things in the world: death and taxes." Maybe you've heard that saying? It's enumerating the inescapability of death. Ancient religions have taught about death: The Tibetan Book of the Dead written in the 8th century was a funerary book describing the moment of death, experiencing after-death reality, and rebirth (Ingo Lauf, 1977). The Buddha taught that all things are in a state of decline after birth, and therefore attachment (or dependence upon) one's youth, physical health, money and even other people are fundamentally futile dependencies. The Buddha seemed to be saying: we overindulge to fortify ourselves from our inevitable mortality. Buddhists have a philosophy about death: you must learn to accept death before you can fully live. Although death is part of the cycle of life, most of us still fear it. When we fear death, we overcompensate by over-consuming. We throw caution to the wind and with it, all consequences. If we can come to terms with the idea of our own deaths, we can live our lives with more intention, purposefulness, direction, and less fear.

Dr. Sigmund Freud theorized, "In Beyond the Pleasure Principle" (1920) that the "Death Drive" was a human craving for self-destructive behavior. This Death Drive was believed to make humans behave in ways which were counter-productive to the self-preservation instinct. Freud further postulated that the Death Drive turned outward results in aggression and destructiveness. Freud also coined the term, "repetition compulsion" which meant to be caught in a cycle of obsessive repeated behaviors. Manifested in "the life-histories of men and women...[as] an essential character-trait which remains always the same and which is compelled to find expression in a repetition of the same experience" (Freud, p. 293). These theories of Freud's seem to be describing addictive and obsessive behaviors. It seems to me that the Death Drive when turned inward, or retroflected (instead of turned outward towards the environment), results in the self-harming tendencies of addictive behavior. It's almost as if unconsciously the addictive self has reasoned: *If I am forbidden socially from outwardly expressing my frustration, anger and outrage, I shall turn it in upon myself. I shall punish me instead of thee.*

In his essay, "The Pleasure Principle (1920)," Freud also wrote that the Death Drive represented an urge to return to a state of calm. His description of the Death Drive reminds me of how suicidal thinking tempts the individual: it holds out the promise of escape from the torturous bind the individual is caught in. "The main importance of (Freud's) essay resides in the striking picture of a human being, struggling between two opposing instincts or drives: Eros, working for creativity, harmony, sexual connection, reproduction and self-preservation; and Thanatos, for destruction, repetition, aggression, compulsion, and self-destruction"

(Wikipedia, 2012). It seems Freud understood the polarity of addiction: two opposing forces, life and destruction, struggling to defeat one another. Freud was describing addiction: a history of self-harming, destructive behavioral patterns. Freud knew it well, for there was a period of his life when Freud was a cocaine addict (Markel, 2011).

Fear of Starvation: Evolutionary Psychology

Evolutionary psychology is a branch of psychology which explains human behavior by theorizing that innate human motivations are actually unconscious drives which perpetuate the species, and therefore powerfully drive behavior and choices. Drives are not "bad;" they are necessary to protect us. The most basic human drives such as: eating, drinking, and having sex perpetuate the human species. However, if unmanaged, biological drives begin taking on a life of their own, instead of us consciously directing them. Over-eating, over-drinking and over-sexing are examples of biological needs which have become excessive and harmful. In "Ego, Hunger and Aggression" (1969), Psychiatrist Dr. Fritz Perls attributes an overly aggressive "oral libido" to an evolutionary fear of starvation. Binge-eating is an eating disorder characterized by gorging oneself on food to tame an insatiable, out-of-control impulse to eat.

In my research of the subject I began to wonder if having been exposed to trauma could trigger this ancient fear of starvation. I wondered this because my own compulsive binge-eating began after a traumatic brush with thyroid cancer. Soon after the cancer surgery, I began over-eating and gaining weight. I blamed it on an over-active thyroid, perhaps hypothyroidism? However, after my hormones had been checked, they reported in the normal range. To make a bad situation worse, I gained 80% more weight when I began a daily pharmaceutical regimen, so I assumed these drugs, infamous for weight-gain, were responsible. However, I began to meet others who were on the same medications who had not become obese as I had. It wasn't until I read this sentence by Dr. Perls: "Self-preservation is granted by the hunger instinct and by defense" (1969), and, "In order to regain the possibility of making contact anew, the task of mourning must be finished" that I began to suspect that neither my thyroid, nor my medication were the culprits. I began to wonder if my brush with cancer had caused me to fear death, and that fear of death was causing me to desire to preserve myself by eating more. Was fear at the heart of my over-eating? Was the evolutionary hunger instinct activated to such a degree that I unconsciously began fortifying myself against death?

Consciously, I understand that an armament of food cannot cause me to live longer, and in reality, over-eating could slowly kill me. Obesity will shorten my life faster than waiting to be taken by cancer; in fact, obesity can cause cancer! I began to see that I had been on unconscious auto-pilot. Unacknowledged fears had been running my life (or at least my mouth). I also thought about what Dr. Perls said about grief: in order to live fully in the present, I must grieve the past and release old "emotional baggage." But how does one do that? When fear of one's death has become real, no longer pushed out of consciousness, how does one make peace with a persistent, unrelenting drive for self-preservation? Addiction (to anything) seems to me to be an "oral libido" gone wild. I've concluded that perhaps both Dr. Freud and Dr. Perls were correct after all: that addictions may be created by the fear of death, and in our drive for self-preservation, we are eating, drinking, or drugging ourselves to death!

Addictions are self-sabotaging behaviors. While we can consciously acknowledge them as self-defeating, their root causes are both evolutionary (self-preservation drives) and unconscious (fear which has been repressed).

To break free from addictive thoughts and behavioral patterns, the underlying causes of the behavior must be identified and understood. Otherwise, we are ever dieting and failing, ever detoxing and relapsing, a vicious, never-ending cycle of failure. At some point we must face our fears if we want our lives to change. We must become consciously aware of why we are being driven like slaves to the refrigerator, to the next drink, to the drugs, to the cigarettes, the sexual encounter, the porn sites, the gambling…at some point we will wake up to our present life and see that fear is robbing us of our present, and maybe even our futures.

Fear of Rejection: Anorexia and Bulimia

How is the obsession to starve oneself, as in the eating disorders of Anorexia Nervosa and Bulimia Nervosa, a display of the fear of starvation or death? After all, starving oneself seems to be directly inviting one's death instead of fortifying oneself against it. For the anorexic or bulimic, I believe starving oneself is motivated not by the fear of death, but by a fear of rejection. For these people, being criticized or rejected is worse than death; they would rather face death than be rejected by their peers or the opposite sex. Evolutionary psychology, a branch of psychology which theorizes that human behaviors are caused by the evolutionary drive to perpetuate the human species (Darwinism) might also agree that these starvation disorders are rooted in an evolutionary fear of rejection. After all, the human "need to belong" is accepted in contemporary psychology as a basic motivational human need (Maslow, 1943). Perhaps these starvation disorders are caused by an ancient need to belong to the group, and not be rejected and left out "on the fray." If Anorexia and Bulimia are caused by a fundamental fear of rejection, and not by the fear of death or starvation, can these "starvation-addicts" resolve their problem of seeking acceptance?

"Retroflexion" is a Gestalt therapy term which means blaming and punishing ourselves instead of turning our anger and aggression outward towards others. Starving oneself is the opposite of gorging oneself. Compulsive over-eaters binge to unconsciously fortify themselves from starvation. Anorexics and Bulimics do just the opposite: they punish and deprive themselves of food because of an unconscious belief that they are "not good enough," believing that being thinner will magically make them feel "good enough" again. More afraid of what others think of them than they are of death, the eating disordered person's fear of death bows to the greater fear of rejection. They would rather chance death than be unacceptable and rejected.

Body dysmorphia (those who see themselves as "fat" or ugly when in reality they are not) sets in as repeated thoughts and behaviors of binging and purging (Bulimia) and avoidance of food (Anorexia) become deeply entrenched behaviors. Self-image becomes defiled and warped and are no longer based in reality; they see a thin, elegant swan instead of the emaciated, 90-pound ugly duckling they have really become. Without psychological intervention, these patients grow gravely ill, and eventually starve themselves to death, just as the obese will "eat themselves to death." While Anorexics and Bulimics fear rejection, the obese fear extinction. The addictive and obsessive exercises included in this workbook can be applied for any type of eating disorder, as well as to other addictive and obsessive behaviors.

Self-Intervention Exercise: Accepting Death

"Instant Death"

Relax by closing your eyes and reclining. Visualize and imagine dying instantly, as in a car-crash, heart-attack, or a stroke. Imagine yourself rising out of your body and surveying the crash site. See your body below. Realize you are still alive, just in spirit form. See the people at the scene and what they are doing. Whatever your feelings, allow yourself to fully feel them. Answer these questions:

1. Are you calm and peaceful?

2. Are you frightened or confused?

3. Are you sad and lonely?

4. What do you want to say, or wish you could say?

"Slow Death"

Visualize yourself dying slowly of cancer, or AIDS, or some other chronic disease. See the attendant medical personnel, and family and friends at your bedside. See their concern, care, and expressions of love. Answer these questions:

1. Imagine being able to finally accept your death as a natural, inevitable part of life. What wisdom would you give to the people around you?

2. Hear what your family members and friends have to say to you as they say their goodbyes. What you would say to them? What requests would you have of them as you say your goodbyes?

3. Visualize yourself dying and releasing the hold you have had on this body and life. What parting thought would you leave with the world?

Self-Intervention: Absolute Thinking

Death is so frightening for us because we cannot imagine "not being." We are genetically programmed to fight for our survival. The idea of death runs contrary to our ego's belief in immortality. One way to regain the feeling of control over our lives is by indulging in "Absolute Thinking." Thinking in black-and white terms, "all-or-nothing" allows us to feel in control, because it promises predictability. Example: "I'm going to eat as little as possible. That way, I'll be accepted." However, the reality is usually different than the "all-or-nothing" thinking promises. The individual may starve herself only to find she isn't "liked" or accepted any differently. Or she may find that although she has more dates when she is thinner, her "sense of self" has begun to depend upon approval from her dates, and not from her own sense of self-worth. The individual, experiencing a lack of control in her life, responds by placing stricter restrictions on herself to feel in control again. Need for control results in absolute thinking, rather than a balanced perspective about her weight. Absolute Thinking is a dead-end strategy, because while it seems she is gaining ground, she is becoming emotionally "malnourished." The individual's body and behavior may interrupt them with messages about being emotionally malnourished; the body 'talks' about that dilemma. When we don't listen to the "body-speak," we develop the following: low self-esteem, insecurity, confused identity, emotional instability, ambivalence, emptiness, meaninglessness, dissociation from environment, confusion, weakness, fear of doing what has been forbidden, and despair.

Self-Intervention Exercise: Absolutisms

A. Describe how past events have led to expecting perfectionism or rigid rules for yourself:

B. Describe what "rules" you have made for yourself, and the pro's and con's of Absolute Thinking:

Chapter 2: Detox Your Thoughts

Emotional Thinking

Negative thinking patterns are the cause of dysfunctional coping strategies. Thinking negatively is toxic, especially if we're already feeling down. It's a serious block to our happiness. The longer we listen to the negative reports the more hopeless we become, leading to a downward spiral in thought, such as: "I'll never be any good", "I'll never find a job" or "I'll never find a partner." These can lead to loss of confidence, anxiety or even depression. A similar type of destructive, self-focused thinking is comparing ourselves to others. "He's richer", "she's thinner" or "he's got a bigger house", and so on. We're surrounded by images of the rich and famous, so much so we forget they're not the average citizen.

Addictive and compulsive thinking isn't logical; it is emotional. Because of this, you cannot "reason" with these drives. Most of them defy logic because they occur unconsciously, out of our conscious awareness. When asked to explain the behaviors, we cannot account for the grip they have upon our lives. Imagine a parent informs a toddler they are taking away his tattered and worn "blankie" because he is too old for it any longer. He will argue and may even fly into an indignant rage; he may become panic stricken when his token and symbol of security and comfort has been denied him. Instinctively he feels the cruelty and injustice of this act. He feels the immediate void, the loss of reassurance, the loss of the "drummed up" safety and familiarity which he had attributed to his "blankie." Similarly, addictive and obsessive behaviors are deeply felt, defy logic, and trigger a visceral response when denied.

The following is a list of emotional symptoms of withdrawal from an addictive substance or compulsive behavior:

Emotional Symptoms of Withdrawal

1. Panic: Crying, outbursts of emotion

2. Disorientation: "Lost" feeling, feeling of a "void" or emptiness

3. Anger: Frustration and rage, blaming, projecting

4. Vulnerability: Feeling weak physically, psychologically and morally. Feeling defeated because of a history of failure

5. Powerlessness: Feelings of helplessness against the drive. Victim mentality; perceiving oneself as helpless to beat it

6. Dissociation: Mild to severe "out of body" experience, feeling you are observing and not "in the moment"

7. Confusion: Don't know what else to do, how else to react

8. Loss of Concentration: Loss of focus and attention to environment

9. Sadness: Experience of grief/loss. Recognition of personal suffering, and identification with others suffering

10. Depression: Overwhelmed by feelings of low self-esteem, worthlessness, defeat, hopelessness

11. Anxiety: Worry, fear, dread, perseveration on problems instead of solutions (catastrophic expectations)

12. Paranoia: Me vs. them mentality, blame-shifting

13. Suicidal Ideation: Giving up on oneself and life. Accepting defeat. Believing we are powerless to change. Believing the world would be better off without us.

For most people there is a never-ending dialogue that goes on in the mind that keeps negative beliefs alive. Every time we do something wrong, or something bad happens, the negative self-talk confirms our beliefs: "I'm a failure as a parent…a partner…I can't ever get it right." The addicted or obsessive person usually chooses to accept one interpretation: it is their fault, they could have prevented it, and they should have done better. This voice I like to call the "Slave Master." The more we listen to it, the deeper the belief becomes entrenched.

Self-Intervention Exercise: MOUNTAIN of STRESS

This workbook and the accompanying workshop training serves as a Stress Inoculation Training—it teaches anxiety reduction techniques and coping skills to reduce addictive and trauma symptoms, and helps correct inaccurate thoughts related to the trauma. The American Psychological Association has published "Stress in America: Our Health at Risk," which explains the impact of stress, and stress according to gender, age and national regions. It can be found at: http://www.apa.org/news/press/releases/stress/2011/final-2011.pdf

Below is an example of the author's line graph showing her 15 individual points of stress on the graph. By connecting each data point with a line, you're able to see the overall stress trends. Use the next graph to plot your stress levels.

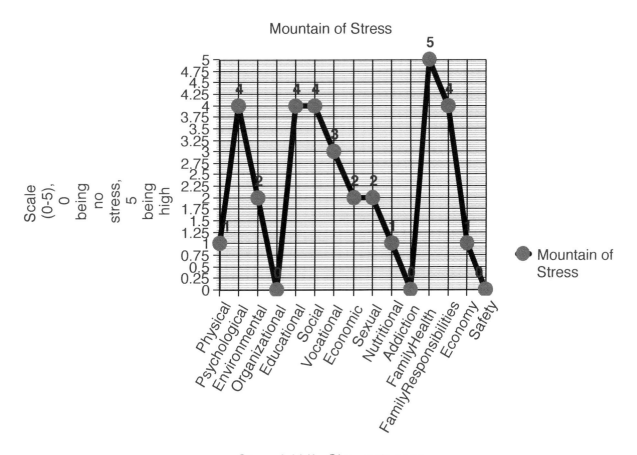

Stressful Life Circumstances

Nina Bingham, 2012

Factors to Chart: Personal Physical Stress (physical illnesses or injury), Psychological Stress (Diagnosis or Symptoms), Environmental Stress (transportation, residential situation, health care providers, etc.), Organizational Stress (Church Functions, Volunteer, Groups), Educational Stress (formal courses or employment training programs), Social Stress (Relationships: Partners, Children, Family, Friends, etc.), Vocational Stress (employment duties and relationships), Economic Stress (bills, travel, retirement worries), Sexual Stress (lack of sex, pressure to perform, conception worries, etc.), Eating Stress (over or under-eating, poor nutrition), Addiction Stress (over-indulging in alcohol, drugs, smoking, etc.), The Economy, Health Problems Affecting My Family, Family Responsibilities, Personal Safety Concerns.

On a scale from 0-10, place a dot on each vertical line to plot your stress in each of the 15 areas of functioning. Lastly, connect the dots with a solid line to view your overall stress levels.

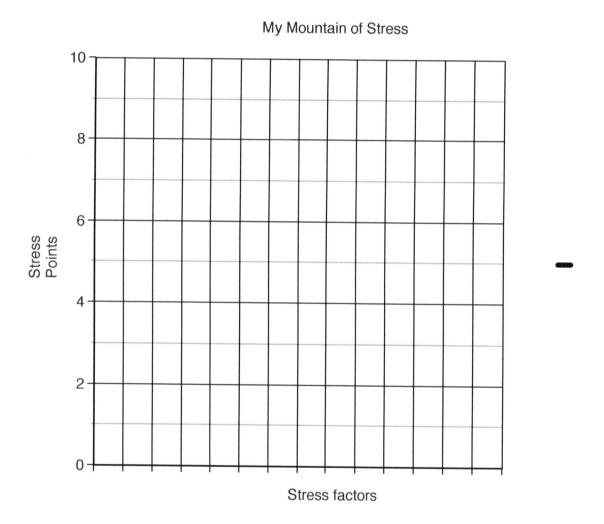

Cognitive Strategies of the Mind

Our brains use a "garden variety" of strategies in assisting us to cope with stress and trauma. When you are in the experience of these, it's very difficult to recognize them for what they are: negative coping strategies. It feels natural for us to use them, and, it is! Evolutionary psychology believes we think "defensively" as a means of defending our survival, and to perpetuate our species. So while these strategies may be genetically innate to the brain, they are not logical, and are emotionally-perceived threat responses. See if you can identify common cognitive strategies that you use:

1. Worrying: Rehearsing, catastrophizing

2. Dwelling on the past: Replaying mistakes

3. Fantasizing about the future: Rehearsing

4. Imagining escape scenarios (leaving job, partner, etc.)

5. Imagining revenge scenarios: Projection

6. Imagining suicide or self-harm scenarios: Retroflection

7. Blaming others or environment-projection. Thinking, "That's not fair…"

8. Blaming ourselves: Guilt or regret. Thinking, "If only…"

9. Intellectualization: Refusal to "feel." Standing aloof, detached, and removed from feelings and others

10. Denial: Denying responsibility for problem, pretending it does not exist

11. Displacement: Shifting of aggression to a less dangerous substitute (instead of yelling at the boss, he yells at his girlfriend)

12. Identification: Assuming the idealized person's actions

13. Introjection: Internalizing standards of behavior and attitudes from authority figures (celebrities, gang members, military, religion, etc.)

14. Rationalization: Justifying behavior by blaming circumstances or others

15. Reaction Formation: Intense judgment against a group of people or individuals which exaggerates their "faults" but exonerates oneself

16. Projection: Attributing behavior to someone else which the person himself is engaged in

17. Suppression: When certain topics are mentioned or approached, client resists discussing the subject, and may show little or no emotion about the subject

18. Anger: Acting angry and loud or threatening to control others

19. Assuming: Interpreting situations before you know the facts

20. Excuse Making: Defensively presenting "reasons" why you did, or did not do something

21. Fronting: Presenting the façade of making changes when you're really just talking

22. I'm Unique: Believing you're above the rules

23. Narcissism: Lacking empathy for others; seeing situations only in terms of your needs

24. Minimizing: Making behaviors seem less significant than they really are

25. Changing Subject: Avoiding responsibility by changing the subject or emphasizing another minor problem

26. Victim Playing: Pretending to be helpless so you do not have to make decisions

27. Dialectical Thinking: Absolute thinking, choosing not to consider all the possibilities so you can avoid change.

Despite the numerous negative strategies, there are **_positive strategies_** our minds can learn to employ more often:

1. Analyzing the situation or others vs. judging

2. Talking affirmatively/positively to yourself, and about ourselves vs. negativity

3. Disputing negative automatic thoughts vs. accepting unconscious beliefs unquestioningly

> ## *Self-Intervention Exercise: Positive Cognitive Strategies*

1. Analyzing vs. Judging: In order to think more objectively and less emotionally about the problem, draw two symbols, one which represents analyzing and the other which represents judging. When you are tempted to "awfulize" and judge, these symbols can remind you to step back and analyze the situation instead of judge it:

2. Affirmation vs. Negativity: The opposite of a negative thought is a positive thought. Speaking out the positive (as in positive affirmations) is key to re-adjusting a pessimistic attitude.

Fill in the blanks of the positive affirmation below about what is possible for you in recovery:

"Because my life holds unlimited potential, I am not limited by the past. I embody the potential

of being_____,

regardless of my current condition."

The ABCD's of Addiction: Rational Emotive Behavioral Therapy

As we will learn next in the ABCDs of Addiction, there is a process for disputation of negative thinking which can re-wire the brain towards more rational, objective thinking, and more positive behavioral outcomes. Created by Dr. Albert Ellis (1994, 2004), Rational Emotive Behavioral Therapy (REBT) is a Cognitive Therapy, or "thought therapy" which teaches us how to think logically and rationally when faced with persuasive, demanding cravings or past patterns. It provides a simple system for "taming the tiger" of your addictive or obsessive thoughts. This system of orderly thought has been used with great success to treat Obsessive Compulsive Disorders (OCD), but I have found it just as useful for addictions and eating disorders.

This system of disputing automatic thoughts is not an instantaneous cure-all. However, regularly applying the 4-steps allows you to test and challenge ideas which are more emotional and less rational. Unless you dispute automatic thoughts on a consistent basis, you won't know if they are true or not. In fact, the longer you try to ignore and suppress addictive and obsessive thoughts, the stronger they become. Carl Jung said, "Anything we resist persists." Instead of suppressing the thought, REBT encourages you to engage in an experiment in which you test the reality of the belief.

The point of the ABCDs is to make you aware of your thoughts and feelings, and the behavior that these thoughts and feelings generate. If you can learn to tolerate the obsessive thoughts without acting on them, and even do the opposite of what the automatic thought is telling you to do, gradually the automatic thoughts loosen their grip, and more self-determined thinking sets in. In other words, you'll get back in the driver's seat of your own life.

The trick is to remember to apply this 4-step process when the temptation strikes to indulge in old, destructive patterns. Some clients use simple and subtle reminders such as: wearing a band around their wrist that they snap when they've become triggered. This reminds them to "snap out of it," and apply the 4-step process. Some clients pull out a picture of a loved one such as their partner or child, and this motivates them to go on fighting the addiction. Other clients close their eyes and picture and imagine a unique, special symbol which reminds them of the healthier life they want. I suggest you find a simple trick that works for you to yank your thoughts back to the present moment, so you can defend yourself against the automatic, obsessive thinking. This thought process can be applied in as little as 5 minutes, and nobody need know what you are doing. I suggest finding a quiet spot where you won't be interrupted, and take a mini-break to concentrate. One client told me she uses the office restroom to go through the steps in her mind!

Rational Emotive Behavioral Therapy Objectives

(1) Identify self-defeating thoughts of addiction

(2) Learn to dispute them

(3) Tolerate automatic thoughts without acting out

ABCDs Example

A - **Activating Event: What activating event triggered the addictive thoughts?**

Example: Co-workers are making plans to have drinks and socialize after work, but you want to quit drinking.

Activating Event: Social Pressure

B - **Belief: What did you "make up" that the situation meant? How did you interpret it?**

Belief: I "made up" that if I didn't go with my co-workers as usual, they might think I have a drinking problem, or I'm being unsocial.

C - **Consequences: What feelings did this create, or what behavior?**

Consequences: I felt obligated to go because they think I'm the "life of the party." They don't know I'm trying to quit, and I don't want to have to tell them.

D - **Dispute: Challenge the automatic self-talk. Look for ANY evidence to the contrary of what you "made up." Are there any times where this hasn't been the case?**

Dispute: In the past, co-workers have told me I shouldn't drink so much when we go out. They'd probably understand if I told them I'm trying to cut back. We have a good relationship; I think they'd understand if I didn't go drinking with them.

Self-Intervention Exercise: Applying the ABCDs

A - Activating Event: What activating events trigger the addictive thoughts?

Write a list of events, people, places, circumstances or sensations that are triggering for you:

B - Belief: What did you "make up" that the situation meant? How did you interpret it?

Write about a time you were triggered. What did you believe about yourself, and/or the situation when you got triggered? (Example: "When I was triggered, I believed about myself that I'll never overcome the behavior, and I made up that my situation is hopeless").

C - Consequences: What feelings did these beliefs create, or what behavior?

(Example: "These beliefs created feelings of hopelessness, helplessness and depression. The behavior that resulted was a drinking binge").

D - Dispute: Dispute these beliefs. Look for ANY evidence to the contrary of what you "made up."

Write about a time in your life, no matter how brief, when these beliefs weren't true about you. What did you do differently in those scenarios? (Example: "When I was in college, I didn't drink. I was earning a degree, and my self-esteem was high. I didn't drink because I had to study").

Chapter 3: Resolving Grief

You may not have thought that grief, or the topic of loss has anything to do with addictive or obsessive behaviors. However, all "hoarders" have something in common (other than an uninhabitable home): they all experienced a loss which was traumatic for them, which triggered their insatiable desire to acquire "more." Sometimes it was a brush with death: a loved-one was injured or died, or some other loss occurred, after which time their propensity for hoarding increased exponentially. The compulsive over-eater, drinker, smoker, drug addict, gambler, sex addict, hoarder, etc. is suffering from grief.

To manage loss we employ coping mechanisms. Obsessive thoughts and compulsive actions are a way of "dealing with" or coping with the suppressed pain of the past. Inwardly we will justify our behaviors. One person might blame past events, another might blame present stress, and some people convert their stress into real or imagined physical problems. Some just blame themselves as "weak" people (known as "retroflection"). However, blame is nothing but a smoke screen. Blame is another word for denial. When we do not "own" our problem, we either turn the problem outward, or we will denigrate ourselves. When we blame, we are denying owning our part in the process.

Grief is a healthy, spontaneous and necessary response to loss. Moving through grief means mourning to reach a resolution. This is called "grief work," and is a painful and sometimes culturally suppressed process. American culture defines loss as an abnormal and stigmatizing event, when in fact loss is the most 'normalizing' of all human experiences. Social support while experiencing grief is essential, crucial to healing, as the process requires validation from others (Klass, 1988). The grieving process results in the cognitive act of redefining oneself, reshaping patterns of behavior, and aligning them with changes that have occurred. To grieve is to redefine our lives. Without grieving the losses, we can become stuck in one aspect of grief, and our ability to cope is compromised and our potential for growth is stunted.

Grief is circular in nature, meaning that it will come and go. It is also a life-long event, because the impact of many losses will never be "forgotten" (nor should they be). To grieve is not to forget. To grieve is to allow oneself to remember, but to release our fixation on the loss. Pain held in consciousness becomes a fixation, where the individual becomes regressed in character and plays the "victim" role, catastrophizing and "incapable" of embracing the fullness of life. Expressing grief is a way out of the victim role. Once grief is expressed, detachment from the past becomes possible. More energy and motivation is freed up to move forward and become empowered.

Interestingly, if we are in denial, we are already engaged in the grieving process. Denial is the first step of the grief process. Psychiatrist Dr. Elizabeth Kubler-Ross (2005) identified five stages in the grief process. If we have been in denial of the grief, the logical next-step would be to complete this natural, healthy grief cycle, and to come to resolution, and absolution for ourselves. How does one move from denial to the remaining four steps? Let's review the grief process to assess which step you are in.

5 Steps of Grief

Step 1 - Denial: Deny the existence of the addiction or obsession. Refusal to accept facts, justification, excuses or blaming as to why it happens.

Step 2 - Anger: Anger occurs when the pattern of addiction or compulsive rituals have been interrupted or denied. The client becomes angry at others and with themselves. The ideal outcome is to learn to discharge and express anger safely and in a healthy way, instead of turning anger outwards (blaming, projection or displacement), or inward upon ourselves (retroflection, such as seen in Anorexia and Bulimia), or channeling it into other more socially-acceptable outlets (such as "shopping therapy").

Step 3 - Bargaining: The hope that the individual can somehow manage the problem alone. When we are in the bargaining step, we are willing to compromise our goals and integrity so we can "deal with the devil." We are willing in our moments of needy desperation to haggle, bargain and manipulate so we can at least get a "piece of the action." Yet in the end, bargaining is the least satisfying of the 5 grief steps, because it is only a quick-fix. In bargaining, the addict sets herself up for failure. For example, the compulsive gambler may justify his lapse by saying, "I won't gamble all of my check, only part of it." Bargaining satiates the itch for the moment, but only temporarily. The root urge and compulsion dangles like a golden carrot in the mind's eye. Eventual dissatisfaction inevitably takes its revenge. In the long-term, bargaining with the addiction just leaves us wanting more; it's just a tease that leaves us hungrier than ever.

Step 4 - Depression: The grieving individual may become withdrawn, quiet, and disconnected from family and friends. They may sleep excessively, skip work, and feel overwhelmed with feelings of helplessness and hopelessness. It is as if the reality of their situation has finally set in. They may even contemplate suicide. I heard it said that there are only two times that we ever change: (1) when it hurts badly enough, or (2) when we have enough education that we choose to change. Pain is a powerful change agent, and so is education. When the individual is in such distress that the only option seems to be suicide, it's time to find help. Calling a mental healthcare professional can be one of the most important calls you'll ever make, and one that not only can save your life, but enable you to find ways to solve the significant problems in your life. If you think you might be depressed, find a mental healthcare professional to talk with, because the truth is: you're just one step away from Step #5-Acceptance. That's where you take the power back, and life gets exciting again.

Step 5 - Acceptance: Individuals begin to make statements such as, "I'm going to get through this," or, "I can't fight it, I may as well deal with it." In this final stage, people begin to come to terms with their situation and the losses they have incurred. There is a resignation to "what is." They begin to realize there is a light at the end of the tunnel; they may feel a renewed sense of hope.

Symptoms of Grief

1. Sadness-Crying, loss of interest

2. Anger-Displaced anger directed at others or inward

3. Irritability-Easily frustrated

4. Survivor Guilt-Regrets about living while another did not

5. Anxiety/Insecurity/Fear-Shaken sense of self-advocacy

6. Abandonment-Feeling lost, directionless, self-pity

7. Loneliness-A void is created in life

8. Yearning-Re-living the past through story-telling, retrospective character develops

9. Powerlessness-Feeling disempowered, helpless feelings

10. Numbness-"Not caring," not knowing how you feel

11. Turmoil-Disorganization, forgetfulness, confusion

12. Depression-Fatigue, low energy, withdrawal, hopelessness, sleep disturbances, avoiding socialization, absentmindedness, confusion, inability to be decisive.

Self-Intervention Exercise: Working Through Grief

Step 1 - Denial: Write a statement accepting responsibility for your dysfunctional behavior:

Example: "I acknowledge the existence of my addiction or obsession. I make a conscious choice to no longer fight facts, justify my behavior, excuse it or blame anyone else for it."

Step 2 - Anger: Write a statement that expresses your commitment to learn to express anger safely and in a healthy way, instead of turning anger outwards onto others or inward upon yourself:

Step 3 - Bargaining: Write a statement that affirms your willingness to get the support you need, and your willingness to set boundaries for yourself. Express your refusal to compromise your goals and integrity:

Step 4 - Depression: Write a promise to yourself and your supporters to reach out instead of withdraw, to not become distant and disconnected from family and friends when you're feeling depressed:

Chapter 4: Just Me and My Trauma

Addictions and obsessions are a method of coping with psychological stress and pain. And, the greater the exposure has been to stress, trauma, abuse and pain, the more severe our symptoms can be. Trauma is not defined by what occurs as much as how we experienced what occurred. What may be traumatic for one person might not be perceived as trauma by the next. A universal defining element of trauma is that it produces emotional and physical distress. Experiencing a traumatic event is not rare. About 60% of men and 50% of women are exposed to a traumatic event in their lifetime. Half of these reported multiple exposures to trauma. Traumas are underreported, so these numbers are low estimates.

Stress can reactivate unresolved psychological conflicts, or "old wounds." Stress is the trigger for re-engaging old feelings of victimization. People who have been traumatized share common feelings, such as: anxiety, depression, anger, fear, betrayal, disappointment, guilt or shame, disbelief, anger, isolation, feeling victimized or violated, insecurity, feeling unsafe, distrust, and a sense of some responsibility for the incident or event. Other reactions may include intrusive thoughts about the event, nightmares, sleep disturbances, feeling jumpy or "on guard," and concentration difficulties. Some people have difficulties in relationships, sexual difficulties, and may even think of suicide or self-harm. Individuals with PTSD are 6 times more likely to attempt suicide.

Post-Traumatic Stress Disorder (PTSD), a diagnosis of severe trauma, has been associated with higher levels of anger and hostility. Anger is the result of having been hurt. Think about it: the last time you hit your head, your automatic reaction (after the, "Ouch!") may have been anger. Anger always follows the more fundamental feeling of rejection or betrayal. Anger can cause a domino-effect of poor decision-making, dismissal from jobs, relationship troubles, etc. Although anger is a natural emotion and must be expressed in order for a person to be emotionally healthy, how we express it is very important. Trauma survivors therefore must learn extraordinary coping and communication skills. The link between addictions, obsessive/compulsive behaviors, eating disorders and trauma has been documented by research. In other words, trauma tends to create unhealthy coping patterns. We use unhealthy methods to rid ourselves of: anxiety, depression, grief, numbness, nervous energy, anger, guilt, physical pain, insomnia, and traumatic memories, among others. While our coping method of choice temporarily pacifies our needs, it prevents: self-awareness, personal growth, impairs our ability to recognize dangerous situations, removes our inhibitions (and the boundaries we had set), and impairs our ability to escape unhealthy people and places. In short, it controls us.

Sometimes, anger or a thirst for revenge may be the only thing that is still keeping us "connected" to our past. When we refuse to forgive, we are refusing to bring closure to the past. This may be because we unconsciously fear we won't be connected any longer to the person who hurt us, or to our childhood. Being unwilling to forgive others may also be a means of avoiding forgiving ourselves as well. Forgiving others may mean having to accept the reality that I am not perfect, either. Sometimes that is a bitter pill to swallow, especially if we have felt we were the "victim." Part of us may want to go on blaming. Forgiveness takes away the victim status, making us responsible for our own happiness. If we haven't offered forgiveness, we keep creating an identity around our pain. I heard a definition of forgiveness I really like: Forgiveness is simply the refusal to hurt the person that hurt you.

By consciously engaging with the trauma memory, the individual learns that it isn't necessary to avoid or deny the traumatic reminder. You might have heard the saying, "Forgive and forget?" That is suppression, and it's a self-destructive way to handle resentment. Forgiving someone doesn't mean you have to pretend like it didn't happen. You can forgive them and remember.

Self-Intervention Exercise: Forgive and Remember

"I feel_____

when you (action)_____

because it makes me/made me feel like_____."

Make your request:

"So my request is that you (action) _____."

Express your commitment to move past the hurts which you sustained:

_____.

Self-Intervention: Resolving Regrets

Steps 8 & 9 of Alcoholics Anonymous ask the recovering alcoholic to make amends to all people they harmed through their alcohol-induced behavior. "These steps are designed to achieve two goals. First, they help repair damaged relationships and second, they provide the other who has been hurt by the alcoholic, an explanation of how alcohol caused the behavior" (Sacks, 2003). You may decide to share these thoughts with others who you feel you have hurt, or you may decide to settle it in the privacy of your own heart, but hanging on to past guilt and regret is not doing anyone any good. It only serves as a self-punishment, and you are attempting to put the old, negative ways behind you. Shame is another word which represents feelings of low self-esteem, belittlement, humiliation, embarrassment and stigmatization or alienation. Shame is the feeling of being "broken," that something is "wrong" with me. Shame is often experienced as the inner, critical voice that judges whatever we do as "not good enough," inferior, worthless. The shaming inner voice can do considerable damage to our self-esteem. For some, their inner critical judge is continuously providing a negative evaluation of what they are doing, moment-by-moment, and play-by-play. Do yourself a favor: begin to release the self-hate and self-blame right now.

Self-Intervention Exercise: Regrets Liberation Therapy

Learning from the "voice of guilt" can be liberating. Answer the following:

1. Describe the situation that led to the guilt or regret:

2. Describe your current emotions after re-telling the story:

3. Describe behaviors that are yours vs. behaviors that are truly not yours (what part of the story is not your responsibility?):

4. Describe inconsistencies between your values and behaviors:

5. Write a heartfelt intention to make amends for the larger problems which your addicted self caused:

6. Describe what you've learned about yourself from the experience?

7. What would you do differently in the future?

8. Express your willingness to forgive yourself:

9. List specific steps you can take to resolve the guilt (making an apology, making restitution, performing a symbolic gesture which gives the opportunity for self-forgiveness):

10. Explain how being free of guilt could liberate you:

Post-Traumatic Growth

There is an "up-side" to trauma known as, "post-traumatic growth." Response to trauma can result in either a risk factor or a healing factor. Researchers Tedeshi and Calhoun (1995) identified positive psychological changes as "post-traumatic growth," and they include: improved relationships, openness, appreciativeness, strength and spiritual growth. "No one would wish traumatic events for themselves or others, but the present findings show their experience is sometimes associated with character strengths." Maybe you've heard the slogan, "Get better, not bitter?" According to Tedeshi and Calhoun (1995), "The effects of these traumatic events are not uniformly negative." Growth can result from trauma. Author Belleruth Naparstek says about trauma, "Trauma: that great terrorizer-produces heroes. No one has to override fear the way a trauma survivor does." Donald Meichenbaum adds, "The story of PTSD is the tale of the indomitable and indefatigable human spirit to survive and adapt."

The following self-interventions were selected from a multitude of psychotherapeutic sources, and they may invoke unexpected cathartic reactions. Be assured that unexpected strong emotion is an expression of inward pain. Unless these feelings are allowed to surface, we are mired in denial, and will stay psychologically and behaviorally regressed. I suggest you consciously give yourself permission to feel your feelings before you begin these exercises, and to allow yourself to remember the trauma that evoked the coping mechanism of addiction or obsessional thinking. Unless problems see the light of day, your soul may never know the freedom it deserves.

Self-Intervention Exercise: Narrative Therapy

Dale Carnagie (1937) said everyone wears two invisible signs on their forehead: Please Understand Me, and Please Make Me Feel Important. Everyone wants to feel understood and important, and that includes you!

One way to better understand yourself and how you arrived where you are is to narrate your unique story. Answering these questions will offer insight into how your life has unfolded, and offer direction for the future.

A. Environmental Factors: List all the ways the addiction or obsessive thinking has affected/impacted your life (relationships, work, family, socially):

B. Developmental Factors: Write about times or stages in your life when you weren't involved with the problematic behavior: What was going on at that time in your life?

C. Unique Outcomes: Write about times when you managed to avoid the behavior, or overcame the problem. Answer these questions:

1. What did you do to overcome or avoid the problem? How did you feel about yourself during that time?

2. What does this tell you about your ability to have power over the problem?

3. What character qualities are required to deal with this problem?

4. If you were to title your life thus far, what would the title be? If you could write a new chapter title for your life, what would it be called?

5. Who were the people that supported you in the past? How did they support you? Who could you tell about this new vision for your life?

D. Miracle Question: If a miracle were to occur overnight, and your problem had miraculously disappeared in the morning, describe how would your life be different?

Self-Intervention Exercise: Letter to a Friend

Write a letter to your addicted self:

A. Express your sympathy for its pain and struggles, writing to it as you would to a dear friend:

B. Express forgiveness of your addicted self for the mistakes and problems it's caused you, and others. Release it from guilt, blame or self-hate:

C. Offer your addicted self your unconditional understanding, acceptance and assistance for the future. Reassure it you'll "be there" to care for it:

Self-Intervention Exercise: Feeling Statement

Express how you feel towards your dysfunctional self:

Give your problem a unique name:

(Dear_____,)

Express your feelings about it: "I feel (emotion) _____

when you (action)_____, because it makes me feel like

(interpretation)_____."

Self-Intervention Exercise: Action Statement

Now that you've expressed how you feel, explain your level of commitment, determination and resolve to do things differently in the future.

Example: "I am resolving today to not be oppressed and overpowered by my addictive self in the future. The action steps I am willing to take are…":

Self-Intervention Exercise: Empty Chair

Created by Psychiatrist Dr. Fritz Perls, the purpose of this powerful Gestalt Therapeutic technique is to visualize and "interact" verbally and aloud with the visualized, imagined figure sitting across from you in an empty chair. Purpose: To gradually, repetitiously expose us to our addictive thinking and behaviors. In becoming acquainted with them, we can reason with them, and gradually experience an integration of the dysfunctional parts of ourselves that are yearning to be accepted.

Procedure: Sit across from an empty chair, and invite your "addicted self" to take the seat opposite you. You may want to have something to write with as impressions come to you; it may be helpful to write down what you are imagining.

A. Visualize your addicted self. Close your eyes and imagine your addicted or compulsive self sitting across from you. Visualize your fat self, your drunken self, your "high" self, your "hoarding" self; your porn-watching self; the "broken" part of you. Observe that part of yourself with detached compassion, as an objective observer. Write in the answers to these questions:

1. What do you generally notice about this self?

2. How old do they seem to be?

3. Notice the posture, what is it dressed in?

4. What attitude does it seem to have?

5. What do you like about it?

6. What do you dislike about it?

B. Talk with your addicted self. The purpose of this exercise is to become accustomed to listening to the addicted part of you. Allow the addicted self to talk, ramble or cry, for as long as it needs to. Do not "bottle it up." Imagine your addicted self is willing to talk, even relieved you have come. Imagine your addicted self talking to you. Write in the answers:

1. What does it say?

2. What is its tone of voice? (Is it pleading like a child? Boastful? Withdrawn? Afraid?)

3. What mood is it in: sad, petulant, angry, resentful, distrustful, or haughty?

4. What do its facial expressions tell you that it's not willing to say?

5. Ask how old your addicted self is, and why?

6. Ask what your addictive self likes about the addiction or compulsive behavior?

7. Ask it all the reasons why doesn't it want to quit?

Self-Intervention Exercise: Inner-Child

Use the Empty Chair Exercise format as described above, only this time, play two different roles: first play the reckless child, and then play the wise parent. Counsel and reason with your obsessive child. Most people must use this inner-child exercise, also called "re-parenting," with their inner-child numerous times in order to see changes in behavioral patterns. Some people have daily conversations (via visualizations) with their inner-child, in order to remind the addicted or compulsive part of them of the goals that the healthier you is trying to achieve. I recommend using both the Empty Chair and Re-Parenting Technique on a regular basis until a new pattern of healthier choices begin to emerge. When old addictive or obsessive thinking return, go back to counseling your inner child. After all, children are nothing if not persistent! Once children see consistency in their parent's message, their behaviors will begin to become complaint.

Procedure: Begin with an empty chair in front of you. Continue to dialogue with your addicted self as a mature parent would with an unreasonable child, until you as the healthier adult are able to help your addicted self see that although they've been trying to protect you, you need them to allow you to feel the pain and to grieve; to express the pent-up pain and anger so you can heal and move on with your life.

1. Ask the reckless child to tell the wise parent why he/she wants to continue the behavior. Listen patiently as the wise parent to all the "reasons." Write the reasons here:

2. Playing the role of wise parent, tell the reckless child why you don't want it to continue its addictive or compulsive behaviors. Explain these behaviors aren't helping, even though it might seem like they are. Explain your wise-mind's reasoning here:

3. Thank your inner child for trying to protect you in the only way it knew how. Write that here:

4. Tell your inner child what you see when you look at it. Then tell it what you want to see when you look at yourself (describe a picture of the non-addicted, healthier you). Explain how the addiction has impacted your life. Write that here:

5. Ask if your inner child would be willing to help you become healthy and strong again?

If it refuses, ask what its reasons are? Write that response here:

Self-Intervention: Inner Child Affirmations

Say these affirmations aloud to your Inner Child when you are feeling insecure, lost, confused, alone, or unlovable. Though they may be difficult to hear, they are the truth about the inner-you, and the younger, injured part of you needs to be reminded of them:

- I love you just the way you are

- It is OK to be you

- You are beautiful

- You can trust yourself

- You are strong

- I believe in you

- You are free to make your own decisions

- It is Ok to ask for help

- You are safe with me

- I am here to protect you

- I am here to help you

- You can trust me

- You can count on me

- You are free to be you

- It is OK to be different

- You are free to be whoever you want to be

- I will never stop loving you, no matter what

- I love you, just the way you are

Self-Intervention Exercise: Inner Child Affirmations

Pick the top three most "unbelievable" affirmations from the above list:

Example: "It is OK to be different"

1.

2.

3.

Write beside them why they seem unbelievable:

Example: "It's OK to be different"—I was different and I got picked on for it in school.

1.

2.

3.

Dispute the negative belief about yourself. Use any evidence to the contrary you can find:

Example: "It's OK to be different"—I was different and I got picked on for it in school.

However, now that I'm an adult, diversity seems to be OK; even I don't feel as weird as I used to.

1.

2.

3.

Chapter 5: Lapse Prevention

With the mind ruminating on automatic obsessive thoughts, we are vulnerable to a lapse, or a re-lapse. *A lapse is a one-time misstep, after which you correct your actions and remain committed to your recovery goals. A re-lapse is when you consciously refuse to try anymore, and stop "starting over."* Research shows that there are three high-risk situations that are associated with about 75% of all lapses. Those three situations are: (1) Situations where the person is experiencing a negative or painful emotional state, such as anxiety, depression, boredom, loneliness, or emptiness (2) Situations involving conflict with someone (3) Social pressure from others to drink/use, either direct or subtle.

Pre-determining your risky situations and developing a plan of action ahead of time to manage them greatly reduces the probability of a lapse. Triggers don't have to be really big things; in fact, the every-day variety can be just as difficult to manage. 75% of all lapses occur within the first 90 days of abstinence. 93% occur within the first 6 months following abstinence. Slips lead to future slips, and regular slips lead to relapse. The early stages of recovery are a time of high vulnerability.

A key factor in overcoming addictive behavior is becoming very proficient at self-soothing and calming techniques. You can add to the Common Coping List (in Chapter 6) as many coping activities as you can think of that you already know help you calm. To avoid relapse, carefully identify your triggers and "high risk" situations. When the craving begins, try to interrupt the destructive thought-cycle by applying the following self-soothing techniques:

Self-Intervention Exercise: Cognitive Diffusion

Rather than suppressing, denying or ignoring the cravings, sit for a minute and write out what your mind is telling you. This technique is called, "Cognitive Diffusion," and means that you observe thoughts without judging them or having to obey them. The key is to remember that our thoughts aren't always true, which means you can dispute them. If you can't dispute them, at least inspect them! You simply want to tune in and listen to them, which can sometimes defuse the need to act on the thought. Observe them with a curious but detached awareness.

Example: "My thoughts are telling me to go have a cigarette again. They are telling me I can't manage how I will feel if I don't. They are telling me I need one, instead of want one."

Write out an example of what your mind might say to you when it begins to crave:

Self-Intervention Exercise: Urge-Surfing

This is a meditation-based method of re-directing your "triggered self," and is mainly utilized in Dialectical Behavioral Therapy (DBT). Having the ability to psychologically "shift gears" is a core coping and self-soothing skill. Through greater body awareness, clients learn to notice when they are slipping into the old coping behaviors, and aids them to develop a new repertoire of coping skills. Breathing through the craving (called Urge Surfing) is a method to respond vs. react, and can, with practice, interrupt the addictive cycle. By focusing your full attention on the craving sensations rather than suppressing them, denying what is happening or ignoring it, your ability to tolerate strong anxiety and to self-sooth will grow.

Procedure: The next time you're triggered, find a comfortable spot to sit or recline. Feel how tense and uptight your craving body feels. Don't resist experiencing the "awfulness of the moment." Remember, whatever you resist persists. You're going to get re-focused now on relaxing the body so your thoughts will relax in turn. Close your eyes if it helps you concentrate on your body, and breathe deeply. As you breathe in, your abdomen should rise. This is called "tummy-breathing." On the out-breath your abdomen should fall. If your tummy isn't going in and out, you are "shoulder breathing," which is a shallow type of breathing, what we normally do when we are tense. To aid in getting relaxed, think the word: "in," on the in-breath, and "out" on the out-breath. After your breathing has steadied, and you're beginning to feel in touch with your breath, repeat the word: "Relax. Relax. Re-laaaax," to yourself.

As you breathe through the sensation of craving (called Urge-Surfing), the cravings should diminish in intensity because you are redirecting your focus from your thoughts to your breath and body. It's a lot like breathing through birth contractions, called Lamaze Breathing. This mindfulness-based intervention can enable you to develop the ability to tolerate strong emotion. Using this craving-tolerance technique regularly (on a daily basis) can break the chain of addictive thinking, because it interrupts and re-directs the automatic compulsive thought from an uptight mind to a relaxed body.

Exercise Summary

1. When triggered remind yourself, "It's time for "Urge Surfing."

2. Acknowledge how tense your muscles and mind are by tuning into your body. Your body may feel: tense, tight, wiry, stiff, sweaty or cold, and you may have muscle agitation. Your mind may feel panicked, desperate, afraid, anxious, confused, etc.

3. Repeat the word, "Relax. Relax. Re-laaaax." Continue to repeat the word while Urge-Surfing.

4. After repeating the word, "Relax," get focused ONLY on your breathing.

5. As you breathe in your abdomen should rise, and on the out-breath it should fall. Think the word: "in," on the in-breath, and "out" on the out-breath. Some people like to put their hands on their abdomens so they can "feel" their breathing, and check to see if they are doing it correctly.

6. Urge Surfing is difficult, especially at first. It's normal to feel disappointed because you may think you're not able to resists the craving for very long. However, the more you practice your "surfing skills," the better surfer you'll become. The goal is to RIDE THAT WAVE until you feel significant relief from the craving. Imagine you are in labor, breathing through contractions.

7. When you're ready to get up, some clients record their times, and then try and beat their own records later. Example: If you Urge Surfed for 2 minutes the first time you tried it, you should be proud! You can keep a log of Urge Surfing times, so when you do it again, you can shoot for surpassing your own record. Tracking Urge Surfing builds confidence in your ability to cope with and manage cravings.

Self-Intervention Exercise: Awareness of Universal Connection

This is a spiritual exercise which can be practiced anytime, anyplace:

1. Focus your attention on where your body touches an object (chair, bed, floor, desk, your clothes, etc.)

2. Consider the function of that object; how it serves you, what the object does for you.

3. Experience the subtle feelings of touching that object (i.e., it feels secure, it feels strong, it feels comfortable, it feels reassuring, etc.)

4. Touch and explore the object, considering all of its physical properties (it is smooth or hard, round or square, cold or warm, etc.)

5. Consider how you as a human being you are continually supported and protected by your environment. Realize that you are connected to all things in your environment, and all things are here for your maintenance, support and nurturance. Realize that consciousness is in you, just as it is (in some form) in the object. Realize you are both nourished by the sun, the air, the rain and the earth.

Write a statement of gratitude which arises in your heart for being cared for and supported by your environment:

If you can, imagine what this object might say to you, and write it below:

Chapter 6: Crisis Kit

This is a special section of the workbook which you can bookmark and return back to later in moments of crisis. Choose from these sure-fire solutions when you feel yourself "losing grip" on your recovery goals:

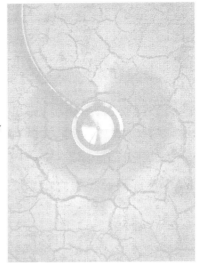

A. Emergency Coping List (ECL) - When regular coping methods aren't effective, call all of the people on your ECL, and talk to the first person who calls you back. Now is not the time to be choosey, be grateful for any support. Make sure you tell whoever is on your ECL that should they get a call from you, you're going to need their support. Add such people as: group therapy members, AA sponsors, as well as supportive friends and family.

B. Safety Zone - Get into your mental safety zone by creating a comforting environment for yourself. Change into your comfiest clothes, get a blanket, hold a treasured item, lock your doors, take a soothing bath, hide in your bed, turn the lights on or off, hold or talk to your pet, but change your environment in some way, i.e. letting cool air in or warming up the house. Next, imagine a favorite place in your mind. Allow yourself to go there, and stay there as long as you can. Take a "mini-mental vacation" and visualize being completely free of the worry in your special place.

C. Remove Triggers - If there is something in your environment which is tempting you to have a lapse, remove it from your environment. This may mean you'll have to get up and go somewhere else, or it may mean you'll have to remove the item, ask the people to leave, or hang up the phone. Remind yourself that if you fail to confront your triggers, you're on a slippery slope.

D. Coping List - Write out a Coping List from the suggestions below, and add your own ideas to the list. Healthy coping activities can distract you when you feel the familiar tug of old patterns. Keep the list in a common area where you'll see it regularly.

Healthy coping includes: Routines, healthy meals, plenty of sleep, exercising, sex, self-intervention exercises, group therapy, individual therapy, recreation and socialization, reading inspiring and motivational books, asking for support from people who care when stressed or tempted, self-forgiveness, and expressing your creativity.

Negative coping includes: Blaming others, blaming ourselves, justifying our behavior or making excuses, over-indulging, seeing only the bad in ourselves, risk-taking behaviors, reacting emotionally or impulsively, or acting-out.

Common Coping List

1. Urge Surf-Relax, belly breath and meditate on your breath as you think: "in" and "out"

2. Call a family member or friend for support

3. Exercise-Go to the gym, exercise at home or take a walk for some air and to clear your head

4. Read Positive Affirmations

5. Do something creative-music, writing, art, dance

6. Think about a healing color: imagine yourself bathed in it, strengthened by it

7. Call on your Higher Power or Higher Self for guidance

8. Listen to music that you enjoy

9. Take a soothing bath

10. Allow yourself to cry

11. Cook

12. Read a book, magazine

12. Watch TV or a movie (especially a funny one)

13. Repeat words of an affirmation as you take a walk

14. Remind yourself it will pass, and repeat the word, "Relax. Relax. Re-laaaax."

15. Journal your feelings

16. Visualize yourself as a tree, roots firmly planted in the ground and immobile

17. Carry a stone in your pocket which you rub, that reminds you to surrender your worries when you touch it

18. Get a massage; get a manicure or pedicure, or a hair cut

19. Record your experiences and feelings in a small recorder

20. Treat yourself to a meal or dessert out

21. Repeat words to a song over and over

22. Color with crayons (my personal favorite)

23. Take a much-needed nap

24. Buy yourself flowers or some other token of self-love and appreciation

25. Light a candle in honor of your achievements, and in faith for the healing yet to come

26. Practicing awareness while washing the dishes-Wash dishes and contemplate each dish as an object of contemplation. Do not hurry: consider the dishes, each dish as sacred.

27. Practicing awareness while cleaning house-Slowly move and fully focus your attention on each task. If your mind wanders from "being in the moment" of the task, bring your awareness back to your breath, and focus on your breath until you are able to re-focus back to your awareness of cleaning

28. Options List-In any situation, you have choices. Make a list of all the options you can think of

29. Get organized-You'll feel more "in control" through to-do lists and a clean environment

30. Structure your day-An active schedule keeps you productive and connected to others

31. Detach from emotional pain-Distract, walk away, and change the "channel"

32. Identify the belief-What unconscious negative belief have you been ruminating on?

E. Just for Today Agreement - When you are in a downward spiral, sometimes the only thing that can save us from a lapse is to "be our word" to ourselves. Although our own promises to ourselves and others may have been compromised many times in the past, in a moment of psychological crisis, write out a brand new agreement, one that is new and fresh, and then read it over many times until the feelings of crisis pass.

For example: "For today, I agree that I will: follow my smoking cessation plan, just for today.

I may not like it, I may even hate it, but I agree to do it just for today. I remember these feelings will pass, they will not last. I agree to this because: I want to feel proud of myself for conquering the urge."

Just for Today Agreement
(fill in the blanks)

"For today, I agree that I will: _____, just for today.

I may not like it, I may even hate it, but I agree to do it for today.

-and-

I remember these feelings will pass, they will not last.

I agree to this because: _____."

PART 2: Body Awakening

Chapter 7: Body-Speak

Just as our minds must learn to turn away from the patterns which threaten our ultimate safety and happiness, our bodies must also be re-trained. Our bodies are an immensely important component of addictive and/or compulsive behavior. In fact, we get "locked-in" to habit patterns because our body's circadian rhythms, sleep patterns, food and drink patterns, and its sexual patterns are all reinforced by the addictive behavior. The addictive or obsessive thoughts become a self-perpetuating loop which the body is part of. The following body exercises have been chosen specifically to interrupt your body's "automatic" response to triggers, and enable you to hear when your body is trying to get through to you.

An important way to release unexpressed feelings that have been pent-up and stored in the subconscious is to physically release them in an emotional "catharsis." When people begin to confront their "demons," they will experience strong feelings. Learn to use the energy of your feelings safely, by physically releasing pent-up frustration or anger. To safely release feelings of aggression or hostility, beat up a pillow, shout, rage or cry when alone (Perls, 1949). Addictive and compulsive behaviors are an outward expression, a physical manifestation of inward pain. When you are willing to stop sweeping your true feelings "under the rug," you may find there is a lot of emotion that has been lying dormant, underneath the calm facade. In therapy-speak, we call this response "abreaction." It means you are expected to have a strong, visceral response to uncovering the pain. Reassure yourself that it's okay to express your suppressed emotions. Don't resist or try to rid yourself physiologically of emotions. Fully feel them, go deeper into them, let the tears flow, let the anger come forward, let the healing begin.

In addition, when the craving impulses strike, another healthy way of releasing emotion is through sexual release of physical tension. Sex can be a positive panacea instead of "acting out." Both sex and exercise release endorphins which are automatic mood-shifters, so if you're tempted to act out, consider enjoying sex or exercising instead.

Self-Intervention Exercise: Body Scan

Recline when alone and quiet. Do a body scan, becoming gradually aware of how each part of your body feels. Becoming familiar with your body's signals is an important part of self-awareness. If any part of your body feels tense or tight or sore, send soothing, comforting and healing thoughts to it. Becoming more aware of how your body speaks to you can be helpful in reducing tension and anxiety that build up before acting out occurs. Short-circuit your addiction by becoming more body-aware.

Write out the answers to these questions:

1. What aches?

2. What feels good?

3. What part of your body are you most aware of?

4. What parts are most tense?

5. If your body could talk, what do you think it would say to you?

6. What do you wish you could change about your body, and why?

7. What do you like about your body, and why?

8. What concerns you most about your body, and is it ok to give attention to resolving the problem?

9. How would your body feel if the problem had been resolved, and what would need to change to feel better?

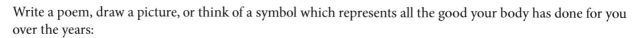

Self-Intervention Exercise: Body Gratitude

Some of us have experienced abuse, trauma or neglect. Because this has happened, our own bodies can be experienced as unsafe places to be: dangerous, risky, or we may dislike or even hate our bodies, or parts of our bodies. Use the "creative you" to express your appreciation of your body as an important, worthwhile and valuable part of the healthier life that you are building. Allow this exercise to be an expression of your gratitude and your commitment to make your body a safe and beautiful place your soul can come home to.

Write a poem, draw a picture, or think of a symbol which represents all the good your body has done for you over the years:

After you've done that, create another poem, picture, or symbol which represents how you intend to treat your body in the future:

Self-Intervention Exercise: Environmental Awareness

Addictive and obsessive thinking is either retrospective, or it anticipates the future. Obsessive thoughts cannot live in the present moment. They always escape into the past, or project themselves into the future. The purpose of this exercise is to train ourselves to be in the present moment: not in the past, and not in the future. Without interrupting the flow of your conscious awareness, allow yourself to repeat the below sentence aloud by filling in the blank, until you have become fully aware of your thoughts, your body AND your environment. See how aware you can become through your five senses. Remember to use all your 5 senses (sight, sound, smell, touch and taste) to become re-acquainted with the here-and-now.

With eyes open, repeat only this sentence aloud, 20-40 times in succession.

"Now I experience_____."

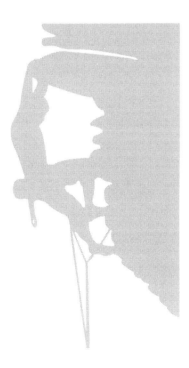

Chapter 8: The A-C-C-E-P-T Method to Re-Design Your Life

The A-C-C-E-P-T Method is a thought-restructuring system designed to enable you think positively and decision-make appropriately. Once you begin the process of sweeping away the cobwebs of old thinking patterns, you may feel the urge to "redesign" your life. Think of it like this: it's time to update your thought patterns, much like you'd want to give an old house a new look. Using the acronym A-C-C-E-P-T as a blueprint, you can recreate your life:

A - Accept. Until we are able to admit we have a problem and can accept that we need support, we're stuck in denial. Instead of remaining powerless, ask the Power of your Higher Self for strength and direction. Some people call this spiritual and universal power "God." Others believe it is their conscience. Others do not relate to those concepts, but understand there is a part of them which believes they can overcome. I have a client who calls it his, "Wise Self." In my opinion, it doesn't matter what name you give it: just call on it in times of need, and be listening and open to its higher guidance and direction.

C - Community. You've heard the saying, "No man is an island?" Unfortunately when we're locked in the grip of addiction, we tend to isolate, and shut others out who might be able to help us. This happens mostly because we truly believe we will be judged, and nobody can understand. However, the real you buried underneath the addicted you would love to have someone to talk to. "Alcohol abusers often seek the comfort of solitude that drinking alone can offer. Alcohol can allow the individual to have some contact with others, but yet to be sufficiently detached, through intoxication, to feel safe" (Sachs, 2003).

The surest way out of addictive behavior is to let someone in. While I think it's wonderful to ask a family member or friend into your circle, the #1 problem I see when treating addictions is that clients resist telling their story to people outside their comfort zone. This is a real predicament, because we don't always listen to the advice of family and friends-they are just "too close." And, we know (or hope) that they will keep loving us in spite of our weaknesses. It is trusting in our comfort-zones which have gotten us to the point of addiction in the first place, so staying in them is not going to help us climb out of them. This is where community comes in.

Whether you like the community you are a part of or not, culturally speaking, these are your brothers and sisters. When you give yourself permission to tell the truth to them, then the cycle of dysfunction can be broken. When you attend group therapy or psychotherapy, a trained clinician is in the position to support you. Mental health professionals can guide you, and equip you with the skills you need to sustain recovery. Many clients with addictions try and fool themselves by believing that they can beat it alone, with no support, and no educational guidance on how to overcome it. It's a little like saying you can swim the English Channel even though you're not a strong swimmer. You might have the best of intentions, but sooner or later, you're going under. My best advice is to find a counselor and/or a therapy group you can attend. Finding enough support is paramount to keeping your head above water. The encouraging news is that research has shown that: "After a period of time in recovery, many individuals start to feel an increased ability to trust themselves, bolstered by their beliefs that a benevolent high power is supporting their efforts" (Sachs, 2003).

C - Create your life. The most powerful words that were ever uttered to me were these: "You are the creator of your life. You are the architect of your own life." The first part of my life was spent trying to please other people, and be who I was told I should be. You know what?

I didn't get very far, or produce very much, and I certainly wasn't very happy being who others told me I should be. To be genuinely happy, you must be yourself, 100% yourself. Once you have worked through the expectations of what other people want from you, and thrown that aside, you are in the unique position to begin living, really living.

To expect society, your cultural heritage, your parents, your company or your boss, your family or your partner to fulfill your life's purpose and destiny for you is to deny that you have that power. You may not feel like you're capable of starting life anew. You may not feel like you can rebuild and create something miraculous and amazing. But you also know that our feelings don't always tell us the truth. In fact, by reading this workbook, you have taken an important step in the right direction: you are becoming more self-aware every minute. There is a term in psychology called, "Internal Locus of Control." It describes people who understand that the power to create the outcome of their lives is internal, and not external. Then there are those who have an "External Locus of Control." These are the people who feel victimized and out of control. They feel life is circumstantial, it is environmental. Studies have shown that people with an Internal Locus of Control are by far happier and healthier than those who see themselves as victims of circumstance. The difference between these two outlooks is that people with internalized direction are people of action. They do not wait for someone to tell them which way to go. They are willing to take calculated risks, and to head towards their dreams, even if they are not sure exactly how it's going to unfold. They simply trust that when they get to the next fork in the road, they will know which way to turn. There is no other way to describe this state than to say these people have faith in themselves. They trust their ability to make decisions.

Here is a non-clinical definition of intelligence that really appeals to me: "Intelligence is the ability to respond well to change." Intelligent people do not fear change; instead, they leverage it to their advantage. They don't stick their heads in the sand and pretend. They see it coming and prepare for it. They say to themselves, "I never thought I'd be here, but here I am. How can I make the best of this situation?" That is an intelligent bird. When we give control to the automatic, addictive thoughts, we are accepting defeat; we are going down without a fight, which is why clients with addictions suffer with self-esteem issues. Clients express to me that there's a part of them which keeps telling them, hounding them that they can overcome the behavior, while a separate part of them believes that they are locked into an unbreakable pattern. In psychological terms, this is known as polarity of personality. All people do not suffer with addictive or compulsive behavior, but I assure you, we all share these two polarities of thought. Gestalt Therapy is founded on this understanding: all of us struggle inwardly with "doing the right thing." Hollywood has depicted this inward polarity as the devil sitting on one shoulder and an angel sitting on another shoulder, both whispering into your ear. To re-create your life, you have to be willing and determined to decide the course of your own destiny.

E - Everyone Stumbles. In the process of recovery, everybody has lapses. It is part of the recovery process. Counselors or group therapy leaders will confirm this to you. "Dodes (1984) reminds us that abstinence is never black and white and the client's capacity to abstain may vary during the course of long-term psychotherapy."

Life wasn't meant to be perfect. If you have perfectionist tendencies, let me remind you of something: Life is messy. In relationships, on the job, mistakes happen, because it is part of being human. Think of how a child learns: by its mistakes! You learned not to touch fire because you put your hand on something hot. Humans learn what to do by first learning what not do. In your quest for recovery should you have a slip and return to the addiction, go ahead and feel guilty for a few minutes, but then get over it. It's been my professional experience that it is the clients who stay mired and stuck in guilt and shame that relapse. That is, they completely stop trying and throw in the towel, due to a simple lapse. Please remember: a lapse is not a relapse. You're only defeated when you stop trying. I heard a minister wisely advise one time, "Never stop starting." When you have a lapse, remind yourself, "It's part of the recovery process. I have not failed if I start again. I'll just start over."

P - Positive. Henry Ford said, "If you think you can or you think you can't, either way you're right." Successful, healthy, happy people all know this one secret: by thinking positively, they draw to themselves that which they desire. Author Rhonda Byrne wrote a best-selling book about this subject entitled, "The Secret" (Byrne, 2006) which explains the Universal Law of Attraction. In it, she reminds readers that whether they think positively or negatively, their thoughts are drawing to them what it is they are predominantly focused upon. If a client is focused on the object of their addiction, they will draw it to themselves like a magnet. If they are convinced they are going to fail, their thoughts will create for themselves a self-fulfilling prophesy of failure. Whether you are thinking positive thoughts of a healthier future or dwelling on negative, pessimistic thoughts of doom, thoughts become reality. Don't ever forget: thoughts become things. One way to combat negative thinking is to regularly use Positive Affirmations. You can find them free on my blog: www.catharsiscounseling.blogspot.com (search for: Positive Affirmations for Health & Prosperity). Re-programming your mind with positive thought can keep your attitude moving forward and leave the negativity behind.

T - Thanks-Giving. All of us have something to be grateful for. Some of us have health, some have wealth, some have family, some have friends, some have fulfilling careers, some have comforting and loyal pets, some have faith in God…whatever you have, celebrate it. It was Oprah Winfrey who said, "You can have it all, you just can't have it all at once." Maybe someday you will have it all, and I hope you do. Until then, make it a daily ritual to practice being grateful for whatever small things you already have. Acknowledging the small things in our lives which are going well for us (even if it's as simple as a delicious cup of coffee) reminds us that life is not all bad. When we practice the power of gratitude, life seems to take on a more realistic and balanced perspective. If you make it a practice to celebrate the high points of your day, your attitude will improve, and people will enjoy your company more. Overall, a grateful person is a happy person.

Self-Intervention Exercises: A-C-C-E-P-T

1. Accept Higher Insight

Write a statement of what you think your Higher Self or Wise-Self might say to you today about your recovery:

2. Creating Community

Write a statement that expresses what ideal community recovery support would look like for you, and why:

Write a statement expressing what you don't want in a community support program, and why:

Write a statement expressing what action steps you could take to find community support:

I could (list actions):

-
-
-
-
-
-
-
-

3. Create Your Life

A. What could you work on now that would make the biggest difference in your life? (Coping skills, medical intervention, communications within relationships, etc.):

B. For your life to be ideal, what are a few things that have to be different?

C. What would you try now if you knew you couldn't fail?

4. Everyone Stumbles

When you have a lapse, what is your action plan? (Removing Triggers, Urge Surf, Emergency Coping List, Chair Exercise/Reparenting, etc.)

A. Rate your level of willingness to find support in a lapse (0-10, 0=will not and 10=certain I will):

B. What are a few pro-active steps you could take to avoid being triggered?

5. Positive

A. What do you hope happens, or what are your expectations? What is the logical next step in your growth?

B. What post-traumatic growth can you identify that has taken place in your life as a result of your problem? (Example: "My problem has taught me to…")

C. What specific self-intervention exercises will you practice to further your post-traumatic growth? (Positive affirmations, body awareness exercises, mind-awareness exercises)

6. *Thanks-Giving*

A. What strengths do you possess?

B. What resources do you have in your environment which could assist you in attaining your recovery goals?

C. Who would you like to thank for the contribution they've made in your life? List them below, and how they have helped you:

Write any other thoughts about your process here:

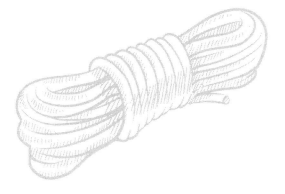

Chapter 9: Reflections of My Journey

You will now be using all the inner work that you have done up to this point. This final section gives you the valuable opportunity to reflect on the growth you've experienced in your journey of recovery. You've had the opportunity to clarify your recovery goals, and have committed to them. It may have felt very psychologically "uphill" in sections of this workbook; however, you've gained some valuable "mountain climbing skills" which will sustain and nourish the new image you've formed of yourself. I see therapy as a "dress rehearsal" for real life. If we were to meet a year from now, I hope you'd be telling me about how you've grown.

I want to emphasize again the importance of having a team of supporters who can encourage you, and challenge you to see these goals into the future. Remember that recovery is a life-long process. Every day of your life there will be something which reminds you of "the old way" to be, and the "Slave Driver" voice will try getting your attention back with his old song: "you'll never be free." Every day we decide who we will be by the actions we take. It is the action we take towards our goals which will determine our level of success in life, so applying these recovery concepts daily is imperative to your long-term success.

Answer these reflection questions:

1. What have been the gains you've experienced? In what ways do you feel you've grown?

2. Were there any beliefs about yourself, or your environment that changed for you?

3. Can you think of a few things you tried in the "outside world" or in our class that you liked, that you'd like to keep doing?

4. Have you seen changes in your feelings or moods?

5. What specific behaviors have you realized kept you from getting what you want from life?

6. What kinds of obstacles or set-backs will you predict you might have? What do you think you can do to lessen the chances of that happening?

7. If you were your own coach, what coaching would you give yourself right now?

8. Describe how you'd like to be able to see yourself in the future?

9. What's the cost if you don't do anything about the problem?

10. What have you discovered are your strengths? What actions can you do more of to further build on your assets?

Glossary Definitions:

1. Obsessions-Cognitive patterns/loops/"old tapes playing." Repetitive thought patterns.

2. Compulsions-Behaviors which seem involuntary and uncontrollable. Unexplainable feelings of uncontrollable drives towards behaviors.

3. Rituals-Overcompensation. "The unpleasant feeling of inferiority must be avoided. A wall of opposites of specific inferiorities is built around the vulnerable spot, the result being a multitude of protective measures, even if entirely superfluous" (p. 67). All addictive and compulsive behaviors are overcompensation or rituals (repetitious behaviors) of one sort or another.

4. Drive-Impulses/desires/compulsions. If a drive is denied, organism goes into "survival mode," and begins addictive behaviors and compulsive thought patterns. Includes physiological arousal, including the stress response (autonomic nervous system hyper- arousal).

5. Evolutionary Psychology-Evolutionary psychologists argue that much of human behavior is the output of psychological adaptations that evolved to solve recurrent problems in human ancestral environments.)Confer et al. 2010; Buss, 2005; Durrant & Ellis, 2003; Pinker, 2002; Tooby & Cosmides, 2005.)

6. Retroflexion-"Retroflection means that some function which originally is directed from the individual towards the world changes its direction and is bent backwards towards the originator" (Perls, 1947, p. 119-120).

7. Projection-Psychological defense mechanism where a person subconsciously denies his or her own attributes, thoughts, and emotions, which are then ascribed to the outside world, usually to other people.

8. Displacement-Unconscious defense mechanism whereby the mind redirects desires felt to be dangerous or unacceptable to a safer or acceptable subject.

9. Compulsive Rituals- A series of acts a person feels must be carried out even though he or she recognizes that the behavior is useless and inappropriate, commonly seen in obsessive-compulsive disorder. Failure to complete the acts causes extreme tension or anxiety.

10. Trigger-Automatically executed response.

11. Coping-Process of managing stressful situations.

12. Body Dysmorphia- Excessive concern about and preoccupation with a perceived defect of their physical features.

References:

Cherry, K. (2010). What Is The Unconscious? About.com. Retrieved from the World Wide Web: http://www.about.com

Freud, S. (1920). Beyond The Pleasure Principle. W.W. Norton & Co. New York.

Ingo Lauf, D. (1977). Secret Doctrines of the Tibetan Books of the Dead. Boulder, Shambhala.

Perls, F.S. (1949). Ego, Hunger and Aggression: The Gestalt therapy of sensory awakening through spontaneous personal encounter, fantasy and contemplation. Vintage Books, Random House, New York.

Wikipedia. (2012). Beyond the Pleasure Principle. Retrieved from:

> http://en.wikipedia.org/wiki/Beyond_the_Pleasure_Principle

Markel, H. (2011). An Anatomy of Addiction: Sigmund Freud, William Halsted, and the Miracle Drug Cocaine. Pantheon Books, New York.

Ellis, A. (2004) Rational Emotive Behavior Therapy: It Works for Me--It Can Work for You. Amherst, NY: Prometheus Books.

Ellis, A. (1994). Reason and Emotion in Psychotherapy: Comprehensive Method of Treating Human Disturbances: Revised and updated. New York, NY: Citadel Press.

Maslow, A.H. (1943). The Theory of Human Motivation. Psychological Review, 50 (4), pp. 370-396.

Kubler-Ross, E. (1969). On Death and Dying. Routledge, ISBN 0-415-04015-9

Klass, D. (1988). Parental grief. New York: Springer.

Byrne, R. (2006). The Secret. Beyond Words Publishing, Hillsboro, OR.

About the Author

Nina D. Bingham has worked in mental health care since 2003, providing individual and group Psychotherapy and clinical hypnotherapy services to adults and children with a wide variety of issues. She has an Associate of Arts in Psychology from Santa Rosa Junior College, a Bachelor's of Arts in Applied Psychology from City University of Seattle, and Nina is enrolled in a Masters of Science in Mental Health Counseling Program at Capella University and is a Master's level intern. She is Certified as a Clinical Hypnotherapist by American Pacific University, and by the American Board of Hypnotherapy. Nina is a member of the American Psychological Association. She is a Qualified Mental Health Care Associate for the State of Oregon (NPI # 1518111053).

Nina has published three books of poetry: www.amazon.com/author/ninabingham

She also enjoys kayaking and writing for her blog: www.catharsiscounseling.blogspot.com

Beginning in 2013, Nina will be facilitating 2-Day Intensive Never Enough Recovery Workshops for: Addictions, Obsessive Compulsive Behavior and Eating Disorders in Portland, Oregon. This workbook will be used as a guide at the interactive workshops.

To learn more about dates for these affordable weekend workshops, please call:
Catharsis Counseling, Portland, Oregon at: (971) 266-0292
or email: createyourlife.nina@gmail.com

Made in the USA
Las Vegas, NV
08 October 2021